THE STARS

THE STARS

FROM BIRTH TO BLACK HOLE

by David J. Darling

Illustrated by Jeanette Swofford

DILLON PRESS, INC.   MINNEAPOLIS, MINNESOTA

Photographs are reproduced through the courtesy of the California Institute of Technology, the Cerro Tololo Inter-American Observatory, the Kitt Peak National Observatory, the Lick Observatory, the National Aeronautics and Space Administration, and the Yerkes Observatory.

Dillon Press, Inc., 242 Portland Avenue South
Minneapolis, Minnesota 55415

Printed in the United States of America

Library of Congress Cataloging in Publication Data

Darling, David J.
    Stars : from birth to black hole.

    Bibliography: p.
    Includes index.
    Summary: Discusses the formation, life, and
destruction of stars and includes an imaginary
spaceship ride through many galaxies to view the
Milky Way and other star clusters.
    1. Stars—Juvenile literature [1. Stars. 2.
Galaxies] I. Title.
QB801.7.D37   1985   523.8   84-23067
ISBN 0-87518-284-4

1   2   3   4   5   6   7   8   9   10   91   90   89   88   87   86   85

Contents

 **Star Facts**

- The *closest* star to the sun is Proxima Centauri, a red dwarf. Its distance: 4¼ light-years (25 trillion miles, or 45 trillion kilometers).

- The *farthest* stars cannot be seen separately. They are contained within the most distant galaxies, which are 10 billion or more light-years away.

- The *biggest* stars are red supergiants. Betelgeuse, for example, has a diameter of about 450 million miles (725 million kilometers).

- The *smallest* common stars are white dwarfs. Some may be only as much as 1,000 miles (1,600 kilometers) across. Neutron stars are even smaller: their diameters are only about 20 miles (32 kilometers).

- The *heaviest* normal stars are the big, blue O-type supergiants. These may be as much as 50 or 60 times heavier than the sun. There may also be "supermassive" stars—R136, for example, in the Tarantula nebula—with as much as 1,000 times the sun's weight.

- The *lightest* stars are red dwarfs. Some weigh only about ten times as much as the planet Jupiter.

- The *hottest* stars are the central stars of planetary nebulae, and the so-called "Wolf-Rayet" stars. These have surface temperatures as high as 180,000 degrees Fahrenheit (100,000 degrees Centigrade).

- The *coolest* stars are red dwarfs. Some glow dully at less than 4,500 degrees Fahrenheit (2,500 degrees Centigrade).

- Among the *brightest* stars are the O- and B-types, such as Rigel, which are 60,000 times brighter than the sun. Some supermassive stars, though, such as R136, may have more than one million times the sun's brightness.

- The *dimmest* stars are, once again, red dwarfs. These can be as much as 150,000 times fainter than the sun.

- The *most dense* stars are neutron stars, one tablespoonful of which might weigh 40 billion tons.

- The *least dense* stars are the bloated red supergiants such as Betelgeuse.

- The *oldest* stars are the dim, red stars in globular clusters. These may have been born when the universe itself was new, 10 to 15 billion years ago.

- The *youngest* stars are the big, bright O- and B-type stars in places such as the Orion nebula. Some of them are less than 100,000 years old.

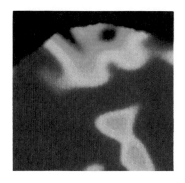

Questions & Answers
About the Stars

Q. Why do some stars twinkle?
A. The earth's dusty, moving atmosphere makes light from a star seem to twinkle or flicker. Stars low down in the sky are affected most, since we are seeing them through the greatest thickness of air.

Q. What kind of star is the sun?
A. A "G-type" yellow dwarf.

Q. Which is the nearest star similar to our sun?
A. Alpha Centauri A, at a distance of 4.3 light-years. It is the brightest of three stars in the Alpha Centauri system, and is just slightly bigger and brighter than the sun.

Q. What is the most common type of star?
A. The red dwarf. There are, for example, six red dwarfs among the ten stars closest to the sun.

Q. How fast do stars move?
A. Stars are so far away that the patterns they make in our night sky hardly seem to change at all, even over

hundreds of years. Yet, every star is really moving quite quickly through space. Star speeds vary from just a few miles per second to well over 100 miles per second.

Q. Do stars ever crash into each other?
A. In most parts of space, stars are so far apart that the chance of them ever bumping into one another is very small indeed. Only in the center of a galaxy, or in globular clusters, is there a slight danger of such a crash.

Q. What is between the stars?
A. Space is never completely empty. Everywhere tiny particles, mainly hydrogen, are present, even far from the nearest star. Usually, these particles are spread very thinly. In some places, though, they clump together to form interstellar clouds of gas and dust.

Q. Are there any stars, other than the sun, that have planets around them?
A. Because of its "wobbling" path, scientists think there may be two planets circling around Barnard's Star, a nearby red dwarf. Planets may also be in orbit around 61 Cygni, Tau Ceti, Epsilon Eridani, and several other neighboring stars. Throughout space they are probably common.

Recently, the Infrared Astronomy Satellite has found large, disk-shaped clouds of gas and dust around stars such as Vega, Formalhaut, and Beta Pictoris. These clouds may contain planets, or the material from which planets will eventually form.

Q. What is a "brown dwarf"?
A. In 1984, a team of Arizona scientists discovered what may be a star that never grew quite heavy enough to be able to shine. Known as a brown dwarf, the object circles around the faint red dwarf star, Van Biesbroeck 8, approximately 21 light-years from earth. Named VB 8B, it is thought to be about the size of Jupiter, but between 30 and 80 times as heavy. It has a surface temperature of 2,000°F (1,100°C). Brown drawfs—part star, part planet—may exist throughout our galaxy in large number.

Q. How many supernovae have been seen?
A. Within the last thousand years or so, just four supernovae have been seen inside our own galaxy. Many more have been spotted in galaxies beyond.

Q. Will there be another supernova soon?
A. In a galaxy such as ours, we would expect roughly one supernova every 100 years. Since the last one to be seen was in 1605, we may be due for another at any time.

Q. How many stars are there in the universe?
A. A normal galaxy may contain more than 100 billion stars, and scientists believe there may be as many as 100 billion galaxies in the universe. The total number of stars would then be 10 billion trillion!

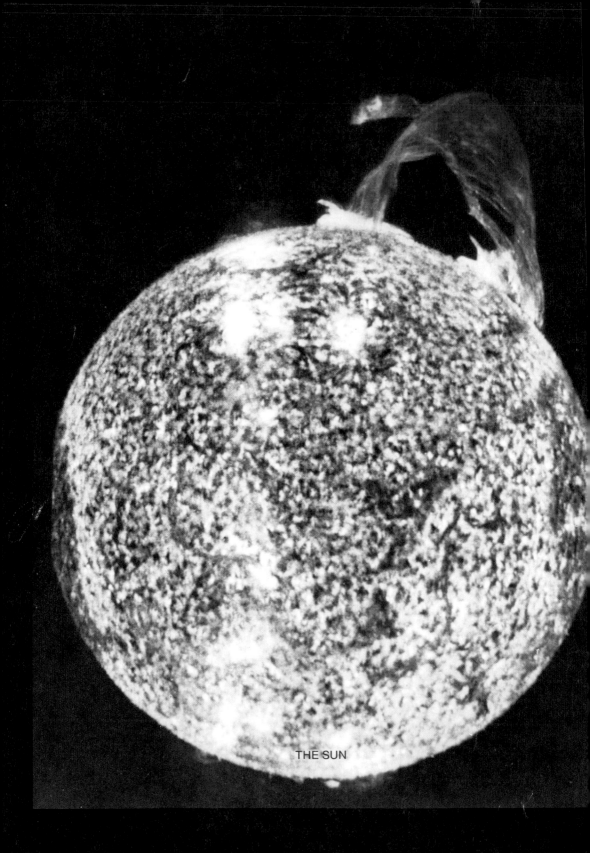

THE SUN

1 A Trip to the Stars

We are aboard a starship, ready to leave on a fantastic journey. We shall see some of the strangest sights in the universe: **red giants**,* **white dwarfs, black holes,** and **pulsars,** to name a few. We shall watch as a star is being born and as others are dying. And we shall plunge into the middle of a star to see how its heat and light are made.

Before our journey's end, we shall watch stars that circle about each other—some that even tear each other apart. We shall see how stars group together in clusters and in galaxies.

Our journey will take us over vast distances. Yet, it begins close to home. It begins, in fact, with the star around which the earth moves—our neighborhood star, the sun.

One Sun Among Many

Like all stars, the sun is a hot, shining ball of gas. But since it's so close, at a distance of only 93 **million** miles (150 million kilometers), it seems very big and bright.

The stars we see at night are **trillions** of miles away. Because they are so distant, they look like tiny points of light. If they were seen close up, many of them would be even bigger and brighter than the sun.

Stars, in fact, come in many types. For one thing, they

*Words in **bold type** are explained in the glossary at the end of this book.

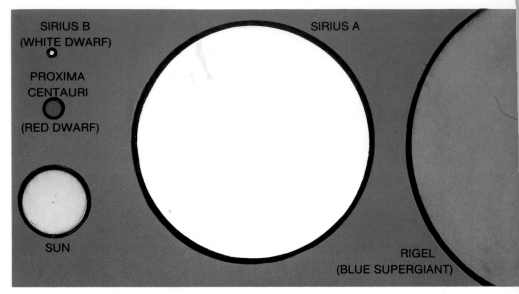

This drawing shows the sizes and colors of some well-known stars. The sun, shown on the left and right-hand pages, is 865,100 miles (1,392,000 kilometers) in diameter.

differ greatly in size. There are **dwarf stars,** so small and faint that only the closest can be seen, even through large telescopes. There are average-sized stars, such as the sun, which is 875,000 miles (1,392,000 kilometers) in **diameter.** There are **giants,** and, biggest of all, **supergiants.**

Stars differ, too, in temperature, color, and brightness. Most important of all, they differ in weight.

To understand just how varied stars can be, let's now visit some that can be seen from earth. We set the controls on our spaceship and soar into the depths of space!

Giants and Dwarfs

Our first stop will be at **Proxima Centauri,** the nearest star to earth after the sun. It lies at a distance of 25 trillion miles (40 trillion kilometers).

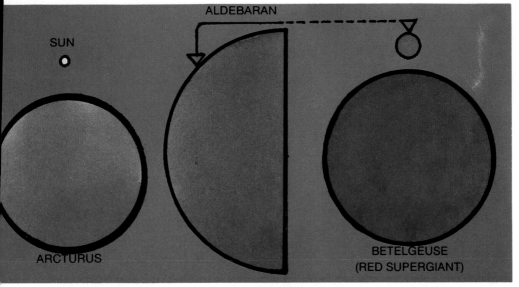

SUN

ALDEBARAN

ARCTURUS

BETELGEUSE
(RED SUPERGIANT)

The other stars are shown in about the size they are in relation to the sun. Stars of different sizes, weights and temperatures have different colors.

To understand how far away this star is, imagine that we could shrink everything down so that the sun were the size of the dot over this *i*. Then the earth would be a speck—too small to be seen—just two inches from it. Proxima Centauri, on the other hand, would lie ten miles away!

Scientists talk about distances to the stars, not in miles or kilometers, but in **light-years.** One light-year is the distance that light, traveling at 186,000 miles per second (300,000 kilometers per second) covers in a year. The distance to Proxima Centauri is 4.3 light-years.

Compared with most star distances, 4.3 light-years is not very far. Yet, Proxima Centauri cannot be seen from earth without a telescope. As we approach it in our spaceship, the reason it is so faint becomes clear.

This is an artist's view of Proxima Centauri, a red dwarf and the nearest star to earth after the sun. In the foreground an imaginary planet orbits this small, dim star 4.3 light-years from earth.

Proxima Centauri is a **red dwarf**—a very small, dim kind of star. Its red body, glowing at just 5,400°F (3,000°C), is 13,000 times fainter and more than 20 times smaller than that of the sun. In fact, at only 40,000 miles (64,000 kilometers) in diameter, Proxima Centauri is less than half the size of the planet Jupiter!

To us such a star may seem strange. But compared to other types, red dwarfs—the most common kind of star—are just "mini" suns. They are small and dim because they were formed with less **matter** than an ordinary star.

There is another type of dwarf star, though, that is really odd. To find the nearest example of it, we must journey to the brightest star in the sky as seen from earth—**Sirius**—8.7 light-years away.

As we come close, we see that Sirius is not a single

In this drawing of Sirius, you can see that it is really two stars. The larger one, Sirius A, is bigger and hotter than the sun and shines white. The smaller one, Sirius B, is a white dwarf.

star. It's really two stars circling around each other at a distance of 2 **billion** miles (3 billion kilometers).

The brighter star, *Sirius A,* is bigger and hotter than the sun. Its surface, at a temperature of 18,000°F (10,000°C) compared with the sun's 11,000°F (6,000°C) shines white rather than yellow.

Our interest, though, is in the fainter star, *Sirius B.* It is only three times as big as the earth. But if we were to scoop up just a thimbleful of Sirius B's matter, we would find that it weighed as much as an elephant!

Sirius B is a type of star called a white dwarf. Made of hot, squashed matter, it is the remains of a much bigger star that shrank after it stopped making new heat and light.

Sirius B is small, faint, and hot. From it, we shall

17

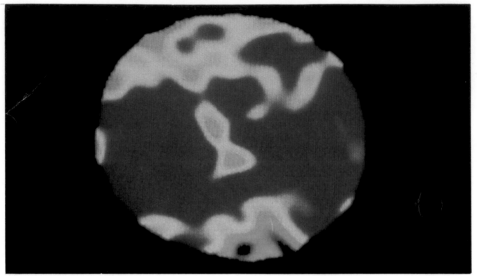

This image of Betelgeuse was made by a computer using a technique called speckle interferometry. Betelgeuse, a red supergiant, is 450 million miles (725 million kilometers) in diameter and a "cool" star.

travel many light-years to a star that's large, bright, and cool.

The star is *Betelgeuse,* which lies 310 light-years away from earth. Even at this great distance, it shines bright and reddish in the night sky. Close up, from our spaceship, it is an amazing sight.

Betelgeuse is not an ordinary star, such as the sun or Sirius, but a **red supergiant.** Its vast body stretches 450 million miles (725 million kilometers) across space. Put in place of the sun, its surface would reach out beyond the fourth planet, Mars.

From its color, we can tell that Betelgeuse is a "cool" star. While Sirius is white-hot, and the sun "yellow-hot," Betelgeuse is only red-hot. Its surface is a little less than half the temperature of the sun.

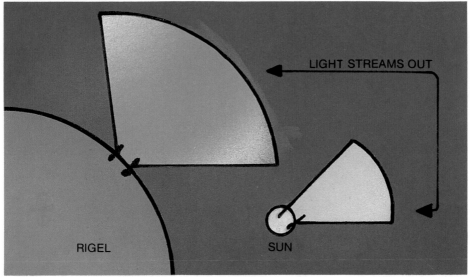

Rigel, a blue supergiant, is extremely hot. This drawing shows that Rigel gives off more heat from a given amount of surface area than a star such as the sun. Because Rigel is heavier than the sun, it will use up its hydrogen fuel in a shorter time.

But not all giant stars are cool. Traveling still farther away, to a distance of 900 light-years, we come to *Rigel*. From earth, Rigel appears as a bright, bluish point of light in the same part of the sky as Betelgeuse. From our nearby starship, we discover that it is a **blue supergiant** —40 million miles (64 million kilometers) in diameter and extremely hot. Rigel's surface is twice the temperature of the sun.

The hotter a star is, the more light each little part of its surface gives off. A city-block-sized area of a blue star's surface, for example, is much brighter than the same area of á red star's surface. Since Rigel is both very hot and very big, it gives off an enormous amount of light. In fact, Rigel is one of the most brilliant stars we know—60,000 times as bright as the sun!

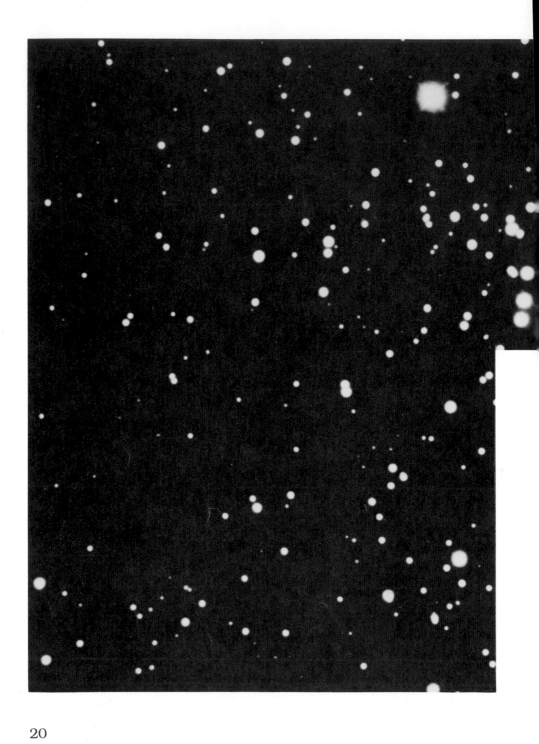

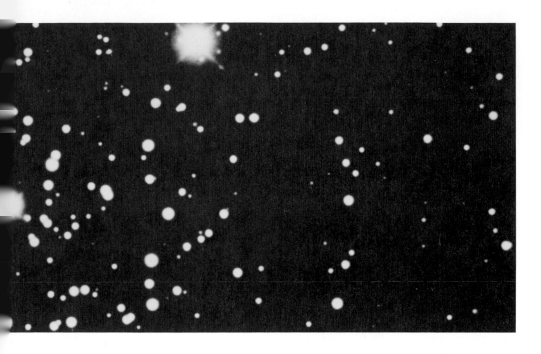

We have seen just a few examples of the tremendous variety of stars around us. Let's now discover where this variety comes from. To do this, we must ask: How are stars born? How do they live? And, how do they eventually die?

THE HORSEHEAD NEBULA—A GREAT GAS AND DUST CLOUD

2 The Life of a Star

As we travel along in our starship, we notice that the space between the stars is not completely empty. In some places, there are great clouds of gas and dust. They may be many light-years across. The material of which they're made—mostly particles of **hydrogen** and **helium** with a sprinkling of dust—is extremely thin. Yet, these clouds are the future birthplaces of new stars.

Let's look at one particular cloud and imagine that we can watch what happens to it over tens of millions of years. Slowly, because of **gravity,** the material of the cloud pulls itself together. The cloud gradually shrinks. At the same time, it becomes warmer.

Now, let's zoom in on one special part of the cloud. Here, a thick clump of material has gathered together. It has started to collapse, or fall in on itself, under its own strong pull of gravity. Its shape has become round.

Gradually, the temperature deep inside the collapsing ball rises. An amazing change is about to happen.

Star Power

Three-quarters of the material in the shrinking cloud is hydrogen gas. When the temperature reaches several thousand degrees, the hydrogen breaks up into

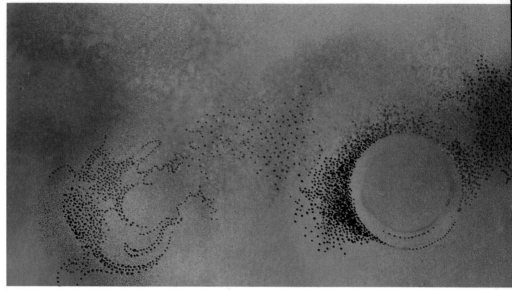

A star begins to form from a collapsing cloud of gas and dust on the left-hand page of this picture. To the right, the temperature rises at the center of the shrinking cloud,

protons. These tiny particles speed around, bumping into each other and bouncing away again.

At the center of the cloud, in the region called the **core,** it is hotter than anywhere else. In fact, the temperature here rises above 18,000,000°F (10,000,000°C).

Then, a very strange thing happens. Protons in the core—now smashing into one another at very high speeds—start sticking together. When four protons have stuck together, they form a particle of helium gas. But they aren't exactly the same.

Two protons have become **neutrons,** and in "fusing" together the protons lose a little bit of their matter. This lost matter turns into **energy** and streams outwards from the core. Scientists call this way of making energy **nuclear fusion.**

24

and energy begins to stream outward from its core. At last the cloud becomes balanced, and a new star is born.

Suddenly, gravity stops squeezing the cloud any smaller. It becomes balanced by the outward force of heat and light from the core. When the inward and outward forces balance, the cloud reaches its final size.

Soon, heat and light arrive at the cloud's surface and burst out into space. The cloud begins to shine—a new star is born!

The Nurseries of Stars

Today we know of a number of places in space where stars are forming. One of the closest is the *Orion nebula*, a great cloud of gas and dust which is a few hundred light-years across and 1,600 light-years away.

Several bright, "newborn" stars, less than a million years old, shine within the Orion nebula. At other places in the cloud, there are **protostars**—stars in the making. They are in the final stages of collapse, just before the start of nuclear fusion. Although they don't yet shine by ordinary light, they do give off **infrared,** or heat, energy. Using special infrared telescopes, scientists can "see" protostars as tiny "hot-spots" within the surrounding cloud.

The Orion nebula is a region where mainly big stars form. From it come the so-called **O-types** and **B-types,** the brightest stars of all. It's not unusual for these stars to be 15 times as heavy, and 20,000 times as bright, as the sun. Like Rigel—itself a B-type—they are also very hot.

Elsewhere in space, there are dusty clouds in which smaller stars are starting to shine. In some, stars about the size of the sun are forming. In others, red dwarfs—as little as one-tenth the sun's weight—are being made.

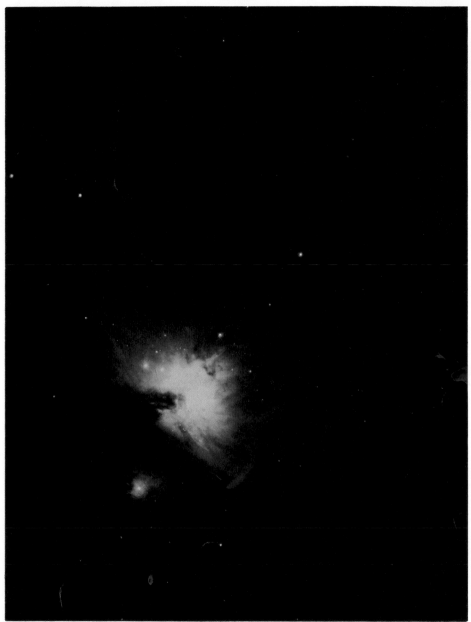

The Orion nebula is a region where mainly big stars called O-types and B-types form. Several newly formed stars already shine within this nebula, and other stars are in the making.

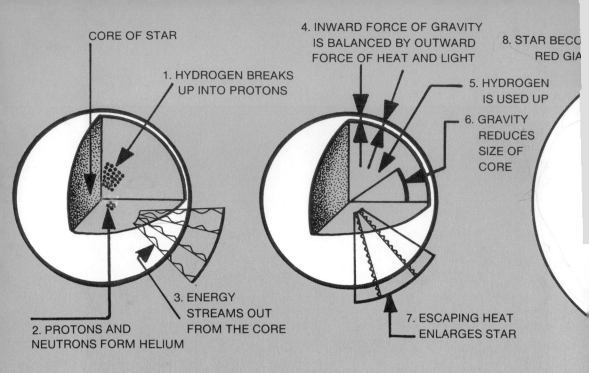

CORE OF STAR

1. HYDROGEN BREAKS UP INTO PROTONS

4. INWARD FORCE OF GRAVITY IS BALANCED BY OUTWARD FORCE OF HEAT AND LIGHT

8. STAR BECO RED GIA

5. HYDROGEN IS USED UP

6. GRAVITY REDUCES SIZE OF CORE

3. ENERGY STREAMS OUT FROM THE CORE

2. PROTONS AND NEUTRONS FORM HELIUM

7. ESCAPING HEAT ENLARGES STAR

These diagrams show the various stages that the sun and similar stars go through from birth to old age. During the final, red giant stage, the sun's surface will cool and glow red, and it will grow to 100 times its normal size.

From Birth to Old Age

Once formed, a star turns hydrogen into helium within its core by nuclear fusion. It enters what scientists call the **hydrogen-burning** stage. In this long, active stage, a star spends most of its life and shines steadily.

The length of the hydrogen-burning stage depends very much on a star's weight. The sun, for example, is now about 5 billion years old. Its supply of hydrogen will last for about another 5 billion years. During all this time, it will look nearly the same as it does today.

What about a star that is much heavier than the sun? You might expect that it would live much longer because it has a greater supply of hydrogen. In fact, this isn't the case. A heavyweight star squeezes its core so hard that the temperature in its core becomes very high. This great

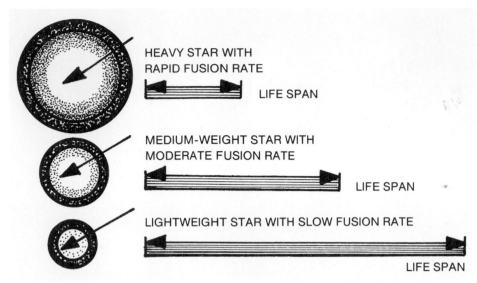

HEAVY STAR WITH
RAPID FUSION RATE

LIFE SPAN

MEDIUM-WEIGHT STAR WITH
MODERATE FUSION RATE

LIFE SPAN

LIGHTWEIGHT STAR WITH SLOW FUSION RATE

LIFE SPAN

These drawings compare the life spans of stars of different weights. Lightweight stars last longer than heavyweight stars because they turn their hydrogen fuel into helium at a much slower rate.

inward pressure makes the fusion of hydrogen to helium happen much faster.

A heavy star—an O- or B- type—may be bright. But its fiery display doesn't last long. In fact, a star with 15 times the weight of the sun uses up all of its hydrogen in less than 10 million years.

A lightweight star, on the other hand, makes its tiny hydrogen supply last much longer. It may be small and dim. But its lifetime is measured, not in millions, or billions, but in trillions of years!

When a star has changed all the hydrogen in its core to helium, strange things start to happen. Exactly what these are depends again on the star's weight, and on its ability to find new ways of making energy.

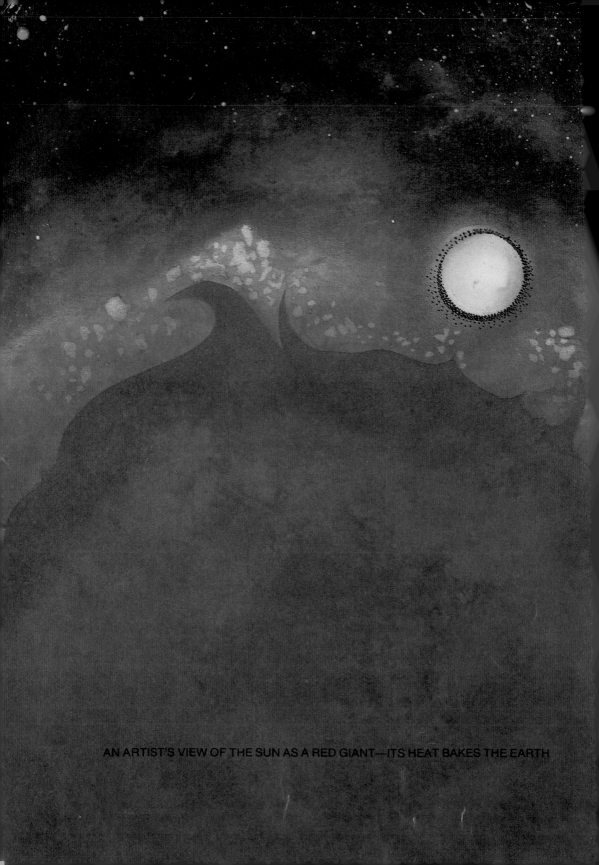

AN ARTIST'S VIEW OF THE SUN AS A RED GIANT—ITS HEAT BAKES THE EARTH

3 Star Doom

Imagine that we are living 5 billion years in the future. From the safety of our starship, we are watching our own sun as it comes to the end of its life. What will happen to the star that has supplied our planet with life-giving heat and light?

First, the sun's core will run out of hydrogen. It will stop making energy by nuclear fusion. Then, gravity will squeeze the core smaller, causing the temperature to rise.

Since some of the heat from the collapsing core will escape from the surface, the sun will continue to shine. The rest of the heat will make the sun's upper parts push outward.

During the next 500 million years, the sun will grow to become a red giant. Its surface will cool to about 5,400°F (3,000°C) and glow red. Its body will swell to become 1,000 times brighter and 100 times bigger than it is today. From our starship, we would see it swallow the innermost planet Mercury, bake the earth, and grow to become a huge star 100 million miles across!

At the same time, the sun's core will get extremely hot. When it reaches 100 million degrees, it will start **helium-burning.** Just as it once made energy by "fusing" hydrogen into helium, so it now will make heat and light by fusing helium into **carbon.**

But the new fuel will not last for long. The helium supply will be used up in about 50 million years. Afterward, the sun will never again make any new heat and light in its core.

For about another 500 million years, it will continue making energy outside the core by using the hydrogen and helium fuel that remain there. During this time, the sun's surface will rise and fall like a giant lung breathing in and out. With each rise it will grow slightly cooler, and with each fall slightly hotter. This rising and falling will cause it to change in brightness—the sun will become a **variable star.**

In time, its risings and fallings will get out of control. The sun will then lose its swollen outer layers altogether.

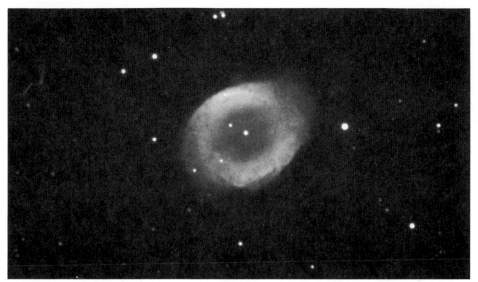

When the sun becomes a planetary nebula, it may look something like the Ring nebula. This photo of the huge, shining shell of gas was taken at Kitt Peak National Observatory.

From our starship, we would see these layers puff out like a giant smoke ring! They will grow to form a huge, shining shell of gas—a **planetary nebula** (which, despite its name, has nothing to do with planets).

At the same time, the sun's dead carbon core will be squeezed smaller by gravity. Tiny particles in the core, called **electrons**, will be squashed closer together. But electrons can't stand to be too crowded! As the core shrinks smaller and smaller, they will fight gravity harder and harder.

Finally, when the sun has been squeezed down to about the size of the earth, gravity will be stopped. The electrons, pushing each other apart, will not let the core shrink any further. The sun will come to rest as a white dwarf, a star like Sirius B.

Stars That Explode

Many stars we see in the night sky will die quietly in the same way as our sun. Having first cast off their red giant "cloaks" as planetary nebulae, they will collapse to become white dwarfs. Heavyweight stars, on the other hand, may end their days in a more explosive way.

A star much heavier than the sun can squeeze its core much harder. Such inward pressure makes the core hotter. The great heat allows the heavyweight star to keep on making new energy beyond the helium-burning stage.

Take a star such as Rigel, for example. With about 50 times the weight of the sun, it will use up all of the hydrogen in its core within a few million years. Then, like Betelguese, Rigel will grow even larger into a red supergiant.

At the same time, Rigel's core will shrink smaller and

The Crab nebula is the remains of a supernova that exploded almost a thousand years ago, in 1054. By now the Crab nebula has spread out to cover an area of space several light-years across.

smaller. It will become hot enough to make substances far heavier than carbon. At last, it will reach the stage where it is filled with **iron**.

Then, an amazing change will take place. Since iron cannot be fused to make more energy, no matter how high the temperature, Rigel's core will suddenly collapse under gravity. When it does, enormous amounts of gas in the outer parts of the star will be shot into space at speeds of up to 10,000 miles (18,000 kilometers) per second. The gas will shine, for a few weeks, as brightly as a billion ordinary stars. Rigel will have become a **supernova!**

Scientists have found the remains of several supernova explosions in space. One of the most famous is the Crab nebula—the glowing wreck, now several light-years across, of a star that blew up in 1054.

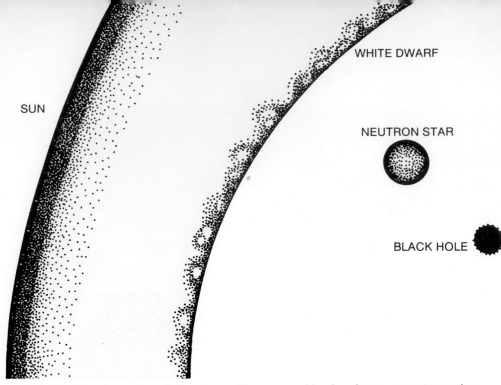

SUN

WHITE DWARF

NEUTRON STAR

BLACK HOLE

This drawing shows the relative sizes of the sun, a white dwarf, a neutron star, and a black hole. A black hole occurs when a dead star's core is so heavy that all its matter is crushed into a tiny space.

Neutron Stars and Pulsars

We have already seen that, in white dwarfs, electrons, pushing each other apart, stop gravity from squeezing the dead core any smaller. But electrons can only fight gravity if the core weighs less than 1½ times as much as the sun.

Following a supernova explosion, the iron core of a big star may weigh more than 1½ times as much as the sun. If it does, gravity squeezes the heavy star's core very hard. It squeezes it so hard that it becomes a **neutron star**—an object only about 20 miles (32 kilometers) in diameter. Then the pushing between neutrons—rather than electrons—may bring gravity to a stop.

A neutron star is made of matter 100 million times thicker than even white dwarf matter. It is so squashed

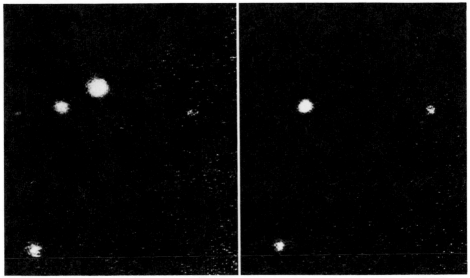

These two photos show the Crab pulsar flashing on at the left and off at the right. You can identify the pulsar by looking for the object that shines at the left but disappears at the right.

that just a tablespoonful of it would weigh more than all of the people on earth put together!

At first, scientists wondered if such a star could really exist. Then, in 1968, astronomers discovered pulsars—stars that seemed to turn on and off very quickly. Soon afterward they found that pulsars are a special kind of neutron star.

When a neutron star is first formed during a super-nova explosion, it may spin very quickly. At the same time, it may send out two narrow beams of **radio waves** in op-posite directions. It may send out light and **X rays,** too. As these beams sweep across our line of sight, they make the star appear to "pulse," or turn on and off. What we see as a pulsar is really a neutron star that is flashing in much the same way as a lighthouse.

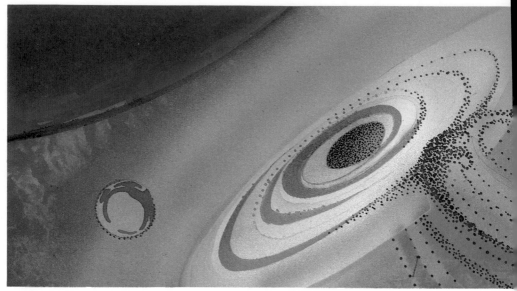

In this picture an artist imagines what a black hole might look like in the center of an active galaxy. Matter from surrounding stars and other objects in space is drawn into

Black Holes

Neutrons can only stop gravity if a dead star's core weighs less than three times as much as the sun. But in some supernovae, scientists think that extremely heavy cores might be left behind. They could weigh ten times as much as the sun.

In the case of a very heavy core, nothing in the universe can keep it from being squeezed harder and harder by gravity. Within the wink of an eye, all the dead star's matter is crushed into a tiny spot smaller than the period at the end of this sentence.

From the space around such a totally crushed star, nothing can escape—not even light. The star has become a black hole.

Today, scientists are still arguing over whether or not

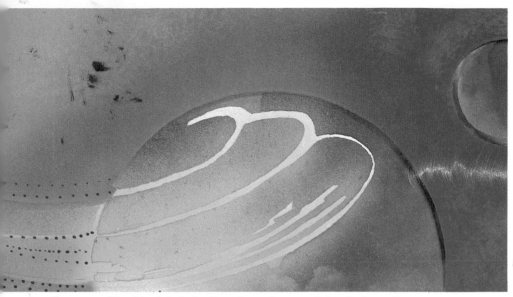

the area of the black hole by its extremely powerful pull of gravity.

black holes really exist in space. The chances seem very good that they do. But black holes are so strange—so different from anything else we know—that it may be several more years before we can be sure.

AN ARTIST'S VIEW OF V.1500 CYGNI—A CLOSE BINARY STAR

4 Twin Suns

Earlier, we found out that Sirius is really made of two stars circling around each other, Sirius A and Sirius B. It is what scientists call a **binary star.**

Throughout space, such "twin suns" are very common. In fact, there may be more binary stars than there are single stars such as the sun. There are also **multiple stars,** in which more than two stars are moving around each other. Proxima Centauri, for example, is the outermost member of a three-star system that also includes the much bigger, brighter stars, *Alpha Centauri A* and *Alpha Centauri B.*

Like single stars, binary and multiple stars come in all types. To discover what strange forms they may take, let's visit some of them in our spaceship.

Stars That Tug and Tear

We head first for a binary star that usually can only be seen from earth through a big telescope. Called *V.1500 Cygni,* it lies 5,000 light-years away.

As we approach, we see that it's made of an ordinary, reddish star and a white dwarf. But the two stars, circling around each other, are only a small distance apart. They form, in fact, a **close binary star.**

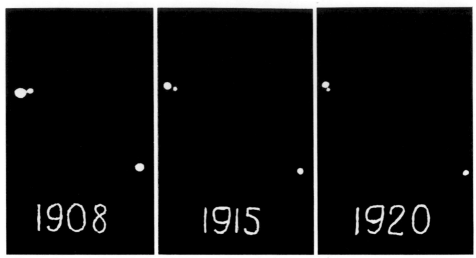

These three photos—taken in 1908, 1915, and 1920—show the motion of the stars in the binary system, Kruger 60. You can see how the stars circle about each other by comparing their positions in each of the photos.

When stars are so close, they pull hard against each other through gravity. In the case of V.1500 Cygni, matter from the outer part of the red star is actually torn away by the gravity of the nearby white dwarf. It then streams across space and is sucked into a whirlpool of hot gas around the smaller star.

As we watch, the gas in the whirlpool—mainly hydrogen—gets hotter and hotter. When it reaches 18,000,000°F (10,000,000°C), it suddenly explodes like a huge nuclear bomb!

The last time this happened was in 1975. Then, for a few days, V.1500 Cygni became hundreds of thousands of times brighter than usual. It became what scientists call a **nova.** In the future, another whirlpool of hot gas will build up, and V.1500 Cygni will turn into a nova again.

Nova Persei 1901 is surrounded by a huge shell of gases. It is an example of a nova that resulted from the action of two stars within a close binary star.

Close binary stars are fascinating objects. Some, instead of a white dwarf, have a neutron star. Again, the neutron star may grab matter from a larger partner and suck it into a whirlpool. But the gravity of a neutron star is so strong that it can heat the gas in the whirlpool until it gives off X rays. The result is an **X-ray binary star.**

In at least one X-ray binary, there may be something even stranger than a neutron star. Scientists think that *Cygnus X-1,* an object 10,000 light-years away, probably contains a black hole!

Over millions of years, a collapsed star—a white dwarf, neutron star, or black hole—can strip away huge amounts of matter from a normal star close by. But what about star pairs in which neither member is collapsed?

In some cases, two ordinary stars will circle about

This is an artist's view of Cygnus X-1, an X-ray binary star that probably contains a black hole. The black hole is a collapsed star that can strip away huge amounts of matter from a normal star close by.

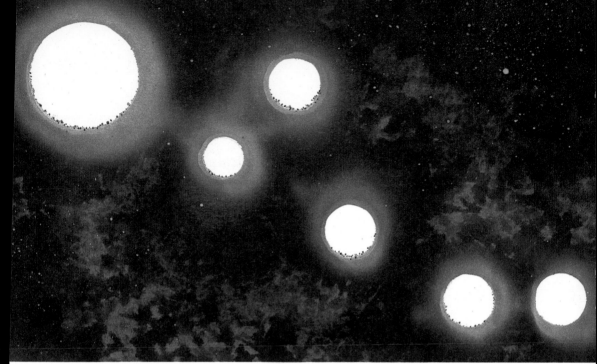

The multiple star Castor shines as a single point of bright light in the night sky. Actually, it contains three close binaries, or a total of six stars, that move around each other.

each other while actually touching at all times. They form a **contact binary star.** Then matter can flow freely from one to the other and back again.

In other binaries, the stars may be separated by a very narrow gap. Approaching *Beta Lyrae,* for example, we find that it contains two stars just 10 million miles (16 million kilometers) apart. Both stars have been pulled into egg-shapes, and the heavier of the pair is tearing great streamers of glowing gas out of its partner!

Since another close binary circles the main pair of Beta Lyrae, this is really a four-star system. It is outdone, though, by the multiple star *Castor.* Shining as a single bright point of light in the night sky, Castor actually contains three close binaries—a total of six stars—that move about each other in a slow, majestic dance!

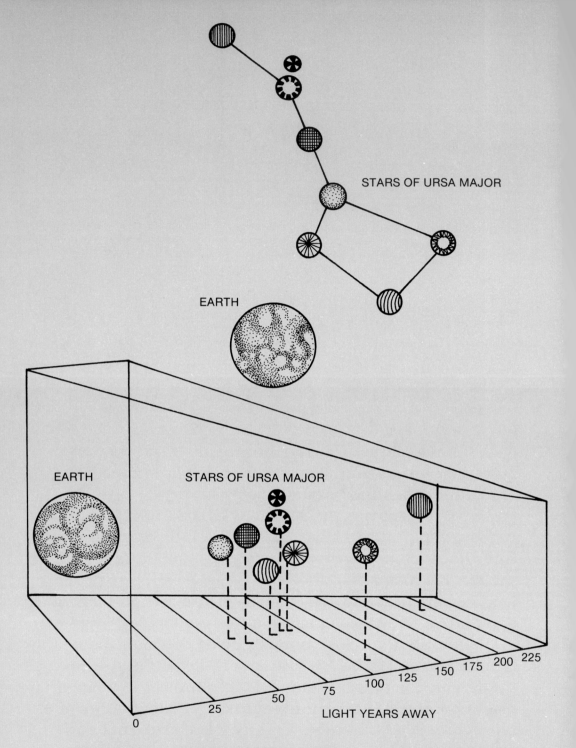

STARS OF URSA MAJOR

EARTH

EARTH

STARS OF URSA MAJOR

0   25   50   75   100   125   150   175   200   225

LIGHT YEARS AWAY

THIS DIAGRAM SHOWS THE STARS OF URSA MAJOR, KNOWN AS THE GREAT
BEAR OR BIG DIPPER. THE TOP PART SHOWS THE POSITION OF THE STARS AS
VIEWED FROM EARTH. THE BOTTOM SHOWS THE SAME STARS ACCORDING TO
THEIR DISTANCE FROM EARTH IN LIGHT-YEARS.

5 Stars in Swarms

Long ago, people who looked into the night sky imagined they could see patterns made by the stars. These patterns are the **constellations.** They are named after legendary heroes and heroines, animals, and well-known objects.

From northern parts of the earth, we can see well-known constellations such as *Orion* the Hunter, *Cygnus* the Swan, and *Ursa Major* the Great Bear. From southern parts, we can see the beautiful *Southern Cross* and *Centaurus* the Centaur (in legend, a beast that was part man, part horse). Many books have been written to help amateur astronomers locate constellations in the night sky. (Two are listed in *Suggested Reading* at the end of this book.)

The stars within each constellation happen to lie in roughly the same direction as seen from earth. But this doesn't mean that they are close together in space. Rigel and Betelguese, for example, are both in the constellation of Orion. And yet, they are separated by the huge distance of 600 light-years!

On the other hand, some stars really do group together in space. They form **star clusters**. Seen through binoculars or a telescope, they are among the most wonderful sights of all.

47

In this close-up photo, the stars of the Pleiades, a famous open cluster, stand out in the constellation of Taurus the Bull.

From One to a Million

When new stars are born, as in the Orion nebula, they are usually formed hundreds or thousands at a time from the same giant cloud. Then, for a few million years, they will be in the same part of space together. They form what is called an **open cluster.**

One of the most famous open clusters is the *Pleiades,* in the constellation of Taurus the Bull. It appears in the night sky as a wispy patch in which six or seven tiny points of light can be seen. But close up, from our space-ship, we would discover that the Pleiades actually contains several hundred hot, bright stars. These new stars are still surrounded by the remains of the gas and dust cloud from which they were recently made.

The stars in an open cluster are too far apart, and too

This globular star cluster in the constellation of Canes Venatici formed billions of years ago when the universe was still young.

few in number, to hold each other together by gravity. After several million years, they drift apart, and the cluster breaks up.

There are other clusters, though, in which the stars are trapped forever. Called **globular clusters,** these are great ball-shaped collections of stars.

Globular clusters formed billions of years ago, when the universe was still young. They contain smaller, cooler stars than the open clusters and are much larger. The mightiest of the globular clusters may hold as many as a million stars and may stretch over 100 light-years of space!

Yet, even globular clusters are not the largest of star groupings. In fact, they form just a small part of a fantastic "star city" that includes the sun and all the other stars around us.

The Milky Way is a spiral galaxy. This photo, taken at Kitt Peak National Observatory, shows a spiral galaxy similar to our own in the constellation of Ursa Major.

Great Galaxies!

With our eyes alone, we can see about 2,000 stars in the night sky. Through binoculars, we can see about 50,000. But through a large telescope, we can see millions upon millions. Some are so distant that the light now reaching us from them began its journey thousands of years ago—perhaps when the Egyptian pyramids were being built or the Romans were beginning their conquests.

All of these stars, and others that are hidden behind clouds of gas and dust, make up our great star city. We live, in fact, in the **Milky Way Galaxy,** a gigantic, spiral-shaped collection of more than 100 billion stars measuring 100,000 light-years across.

In the future we may travel to the stars in other parts

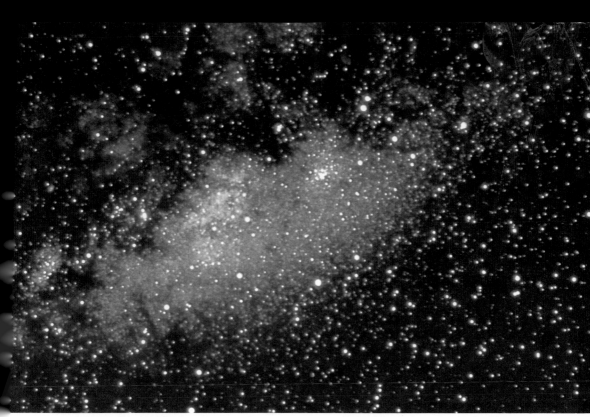

A wide angle view of the Milky Way Galaxy in the direction of its center appears in this photo. It was taken at the Cerro Tololo Inter-American Observatory.

of the Galaxy. We may see them close up, as we do our own sun. Imagine what it would be like to land on the planet of a binary star, journey to the center of a globular cluster, and skim by the fiery whirlpool around a black hole!

Appendix A:
Discover For Yourself

Explore the Stars

With your eyes alone, you can see about 2,000 stars in the sky on a clear, dark night. Make these stars your starting point for an amazing voyage of discovery, trillions of miles from home.

Like any explorer, you will wish to study maps of the places you will be visiting. Use the star charts in *The Night Sky Book* and *The Star Book* (See *Suggested Reading*) to discover some of the main constellations and how these are arranged. Visit, if you can, a planetarium. Then, choose a good starry evening—and begin your voyage!

Some constellations are much easier to find than others. Among the most famous is the Big Dipper, or Ursa Major. This can be used as a signpost to locate other important sights in the sky.

From the Big Dipper, you can quickly find your way to the bright stars Vega, Arcturus, Capella, and Polaris (the Pole Star). Also signposted are the constellations Leo and Gemini.

Even more splendid than the Big Dipper is Orion the Hunter, with his three-starred belt and the brilliant stars Rigel and Betelgeuse. Orion can be used as a guide to Sirius, Procyon, Aldebaran, Capella, and the "heavenly twins," Castor and Pollux.

Another sight to look for is the misty, ragged band of the Milky Way. This covers the belt of sky in which we can see most stars and most bright star groupings. Along the Milky Way are constellations such as Cassiopeia, Cygnus, Perseus, and Auriga. Cassiopeia is very easy to spot: it is shaped like a small, bright, misshapen *W*. Cygnus, on the other hand, has the form of a cross.

From the brightest stars and star groupings, move on to the dimmer parts of the sky. You may want to make a list of the stars and constellations you intend to look for each night, using your star book or chart as a guide.

Keep a diary or "log book" of the stars you have seen. What color did they appear? How bright were they? Were there any other stars very close by in the sky? Write down your sightings first, and then learn more about the stars you have seen from this and other books. Think about how a star's temperature, true brightness, and distance affect its appearance in the sky.

With binoculars you can see many more stars. Look especially in the direction of the Milky Way. Also, try to find the Orion nebula (below Orion's belt), star clusters such as the Pleiades, and some examples of binary stars.

Appendix B: Facts About Some Well-Known Stars

Star	Distance (light-years)	Diameter (miles)	Brightness (Sun=1)
The sun	8 1/3 light-minutes	865,000	1
Proxima Centauri	4 1/4	40,000	1/13,000
Alpha Centauri A	4 1/3	1,000,000	1 1/10
Sirius A	8 2/3	3,000,000	26
Sirius B	8 2/3	26,000	1/10,000
Procyon	11 1/2	3,500,000	11
Altair	16 1/2	3,000,000	10
Vega	26	5,000,000	52
Arcturus	36	20,000,000	115
Capella	42	10,000,000	70
Aldebaran	68	35,000,000	100
Betelgeuse	310	450,000,000	15,000
Polaris	680	30,000,000	6,000
Rigel	900	40,000,000	60,000
Canopus	1,200	100,000,000	200,000

Temperature (degrees C)	Color	Notes
6,000	Yellow	Our neighborhood star
3,000	Red	Red dwarf; the nearest star to the sun
6,000	Yellow	Nearest sunlike star
10,000	White	Brightest star in our night sky
8,500	White	Nearest white dwarf
6,800	White	
9,000	White	
10,700	Bluish-white	
4,800	Orange	
5,300	Yellow	
4,200	Orange	Red giant
3,000	Red	Red supergiant
6,500	White	The Pole Star
12,000	Bluish-white	Blue supergiant
9,000	White	One of the brightest stars known

Appendix C:
Amateur Astronomy Groups
in the United States,
Canada, and Great Britain

For information or resource materials about the subjects covered in this book, contact your local astronomy group, science museum, or planetarium. You may also write to one of the national amateur astronomy groups listed below.

United States
The Astronomical League
Donald Archer,
  Executive Secretary
P.O. Box 12821
Tucson, Arizona 85732

American Association of
  Variable Star Astronomers
187 Concord Avenue
Cambridge, Massachusetts 02138

Great Britain
Junior Astronomical Society
58 Vaughan Gardens
Ilford
Essex IG1 3PD England

British Astronomical Assoc.
Burlington House
Piccadilly
London W1V 0NL England

Canada
The Royal Astronomical Society of Canada
La Société Royale d'Astronomie du Canada
Rosemary Freeman, Executive Secretary
136 Dupont Street
Toronto, Ontario M5R 1V2 Canada

Glossary

billion—a thousand million. Written as 1,000,000,000

binary star—two stars that circle around each other. There are many different kinds of binary stars

black hole—a region of space from which nothing— not even light—can escape. Black holes may be formed from very heavy stars that collapse at the end of their lives

blue supergiant—a very large, hot kind of star. Blue supergiants, unlike red supergiants, are still making energy in their cores by fusing hydrogen into helium

B-type star—a very big, bright, hot kind of star. B-type stars include white and blue, giants and supergiants

carbon—a substance, common on earth, that makes up the cores of dead stars weighing about the same as the sun

close binary star—a type of binary star in which the two stars circle around each other separated by only a small distance

constellation—a pattern of stars in the night sky

contact binary star—a type of binary star in which the two stars are actually touching as they move around each other

core—the small, hot, central part of a star where most of the star's heat and light is made

diameter—the length of a straight line that runs from one side of an object to the other, passing through its center

dwarf star—a star of small size

electron—a tiny particle,

even lighter than a proton or neutron

energy—the ability to be active or do work. There are many forms of energy. Those made inside stars include radio waves, X rays, light, and heat

giant star—a star of large size

globular cluster—a huge, ball-shaped cluster of stars bound together by gravity. Globular clusters are extremely old and contain mostly small stars

gravity—the force by which all objects pull on all other objects. Gravity, for example, is what holds a star together and what crushes a star's core at the end of its life

helium—a gas. The second lightest substance of all and a common substance in stars.

helium-burning—the nuclear fusion of helium into heavier substances. Helium-burning only takes place in older stars whose cores have become very hot

hydrogen—a gas. The lightest substance of all. It makes up three-quarters of the matter in most stars and is the main fuel for nuclear fusion in their cores

hydrogen-burning—the nuclear fusion of hydrogen into helium. It is the most important way by which stars make heat and light

infrared—the kind of waves that carry heat. They are given off by all warm objects

iron—a common metal found on earth. It is only formed in the cores of the heaviest stars, and it then marks the end of a star's life. Iron cannot be fused to

make heat and light

light-year—the distance traveled by light in a year. It is equal to about 6 trillion miles (9½ trillion kilometers)

matter—anything that has weight and takes up space

Milky Way Galaxy—the galaxy in which we live. It is a huge, spiral-shaped collection of more than 100 billion stars, about 100,000 light-years across

million—a thousand thousand. Written as 1,000,000

multiple star—several stars that circle around each other

neutron—a tiny particle made during fusion in the cores of stars. Two neutrons and two protons form a piece of helium in stars. See *neutron stars*

neutron star—a type of collapsed star. Neutron stars—made of tightly-packed neutrons—form from dead star cores weighing between 1½ and 3 times as much as the sun. A thimbleful of neutron star matter would weigh about 100 million tons

nova—a close binary star, containing a white dwarf and a normal star, that suddenly brightens by as much as a million times. The brightening is caused by gas, taken from the normal star, that explodes close to the dwarf

nuclear fusion—the way in which stars make energy by turning lighter substances (mainly hydrogen) into heavier substances (mainly helium) at extremely high temperatures

open cluster—a short-lived cluster containing perhaps

several hundred stars that were formed in the same region of space. Unlike globular clusters, open clusters are not bound together by gravity

O-type star—the biggest, brightest, hottest kind of star. O-types include white and blue, giants and super-giants

planetary nebula—a bright ring, or shell, of gas thrown off by stars similar to the sun in their old age

proton—a tiny particle. Protons, from split-up hydrogen, fuse in the cores of stars and give off great amounts of energy

protostar—a star that has not yet begun to shine. It is still forming from the surrounding gas and dust cloud

Proxima Centauri—the nearest star to us, after the sun. It is a red dwarf, 4.3 light-years away

pulsar—a kind of newly-formed neutron star. Pulsars spin very quickly and beam out signals like a lighthouse

radio waves—weak, invisible waves of energy that, like light and heat , are given off by many objects in space

red dwarf—a small, light-weight kind of star. Since red dwarfs make much less energy in their cores than stars similar to the sun, they are cool and faint. They are the most common type of star in space

red giant—a star which, in its old age, has grown large and cool. Stars like the sun turn into red giants when they have used up the remaining hydrogen fuel in their cores

red supergiant—a star similar to a red giant, but

much larger. Red supergiants are aging, heavyweight stars

Sirius—the brightest star in the night sky as seen from earth. It appears so bright because, at a distance of 8.7 light-years, it is closer to earth than almost all other stars

star cluster—a group of stars close together in space. See *globular cluster* and *open cluster*

supergiant—the biggest kind of star. See *blue supergiant* and *red supergiant*

supernova—an exploding heavyweight star. A supernova occurs when the outer parts of a heavy star are blown off at the end of its life. For a few weeks, it is extremely bright—at least a billion times as bright as the sun

trillion—a thousand billion. Written as 1,000,000,000,000

variable star—a star that changes in brightness. There are many different kinds of variable stars

white dwarf—a type of collapsed star. White dwarfs form from the dead cores of stars similar to the sun. A thimbleful of white dwarf matter would weigh about ten tons

X-ray binary star—a close binary star containing a neutron star (or, possibly, a black hole) and a normal star. Gas from the normal star is stripped off, by the collapsed partner, and made so hot that it gives off X rays

X rays—very powerful, invisible waves of energy

Suggested Reading

Adler, Irving. *The Stars: Decoding Their Messages.* New
York: Thomas Y. Crowell, 1980.
How do we know the distances of stars? How can we tell so
much about stars—their temperature, density, makeup, and
so on—simply by studying their light? In giving the
answers, this book shows how astronomers have become
experts at "decoding" starlight. (Advanced)

Burnham, Robert. *The Star Book.* Milwaukee: AstroMedia
Corp, 1983.
A clear, easy-to-use guide to the night sky. This book contains full-color maps showing the stars for each season, together with a description of the most important objects on
view. (Advanced)

Jobb, Jamie. *The Night Sky Book.* Boston: Little, Brown,
1977.
Stargazing is fun! This is the message of a book, full of lively
sketches and of projects to do, written especially for the
young astronomer. (Beginner-Intermediate)

Kaufmann, William J. *Black Holes and Warped Spacetime.*
New York: Bantam Books, 1981.
A book for the older reader who wishes to learn more of the
strange facts about black holes. The first three chapters deal
with the birth, life, and death of stars, and explain how
white dwarfs, neutron stars, and black holes are formed.
(Advanced)

 **Index**